Reinvent Your Life in 15 Minutes a Day

*A Guide to Thinking Big and
Living a More Fulfilling Life*

Suzanne Wescoe

ISBN: **0986146803**
ISBN-13: 978-0-9861468-0-0

Library of Congress Control Number: 2015902689
Suzanne Wescoe, Philadelphia, PA

This book is dedicated to the Beaver and Wendy.

CONTENTS

PART SIX

QUESTIONS YOU SHOULD ASK YOURSELF

PART SEVEN

IT'S ALL ABOUT YOUR PERSPECTIVE

INTRODUCTION

You can do anything for 15 minutes a day.   This guide is designed to help you think big to unlock the potential inside of you and to live a more fulfilling life.

Every day you should remind yourself about how great you are.   This is your foundation.   You can't begin to discover your potential until you deeply know who you are right now.   Learn to condition yourself to overwrite any long standing negative thoughts and attitudes with positive ones.   The goal is to jump start the day feeling energized and having a deep conviction that anything is possible.

Your life is speaking to you so learn its language. Find out how to look inward for answers that you seek.   It's all about becoming aware and tuning into your inner guidance system that provides information that keeps you on the best path for your life.

Get in touch with who you are and what your life purpose is.   There's a depth to you that needs to be rediscovered. Uncover your inner circle of experts and your higher self to assist you as you take steps toward your dream.

Negatives things happen in life which can't always be prevented.   Instead of getting stuck in a downward spiral of negativity, discover how to grow in the adversity and look for the hidden meaning. You will recognize there is wisdom in every challenge. It's all about turning negatives into positives.

Engage your life by asking questions. When you ask the right questions and you will be amazed at all the guidance you will receive.

Your perspective can catapult you to the next level or keep you stuck where you are. Practice having a positive mindset and being happy where you are while looking at the bigger picture.

If you want a more fulfilling life, then create an environment where you are constantly reminded of your unlimited potential. Get into the practice of breathing life into your dreams.

Let's Start with the Basics

Think about the books you have read over the years about how to get what you desire or how to become a new and improved you. If you are like me, after finishing a book you are on fire and can't wait to include some of the new ideas into your daily routine. You start with a topic that resonates with you.

During the first few days you make a conscious effort to recall and practice the new ideas in an attempt to change your behavior. You are off to a good start but then real life sets in with demands from your job and personal life pulling you in different directions. What seemed so important a few days ago are a distant memory and a missed opportunity to put your life on a new trajectory.

How do you begin to make positive changes when life is so busy and once is not enough?

Repetition is Key

You begin by acknowledging that you must find a way to consistently practice a new way of thinking so it becomes a part of you.

Think about the Olympic athletes and all the hours, days, weeks, months and years of practicing their skills. Think about all the time an actor spends memorizing their lines and countless rehearsals prior to their performance. Consider something that you do very well and what it took you to get to that level of expertise.

What all of you have in common was the commitment and the amount of time spent developing your skills over and over and over again so it became an automatic response.

This book is designed to be your guide, a script to practice new higher forms of thinking and being so you can reach your highest potential and live a more fulfilling life.

Reinvent Your Life by Giving It a New Script

When you combine repetition with believing what you are saying is true and expecting it to happen, you are sending out a powerful message and in time you will see a positive shift in your behavior.

A Wide Range of Feelings

Every day we experience different thoughts and feelings. One day we're happy and everything goes our way. The next we have the weight of the world on our shoulders. We feel stressed and not confident about whom we are and where we are in life. We wonder if we will ever achieve our goals.

To be human is to experience a wide range of thoughts and feelings, both positive and negative. How can we condition ourselves to access more of the positive and less of the negative?

Words have the power to transport us to a new reality. What do you feel when you read the following:

- Anything is possible.

- Opportunities are headed my way.

- What I need will always show up.

Do you feel uplifted and more optimistic about life? What about when you are feeling negative. How do you switch over to positive thoughts when you are feeling negative, stressed or out of sorts? That's where this book comes in.

Use This Book to Practice

Make it a daily practice to read 15 minutes a day. Read different sections of the book to reprogram your mind and to break out of well-established thought patterns that no longer serve you.

You can do anything for 15 minutes so make it count by doing something that will make a big difference in your life.

Start with Part One – DAILY CONDITIONING. Read this section each day to remind yourself about how great you are and how there is a great plan for your life. It doesn't matter if some of the statements are not true at the moment. In time, they will be.

What You Say You Are Moving Towards

This is an opportunity to reprogram your mind by replacing patterns that don't serve you anymore. You will learn to focus on the possibilities each day, not the limitations. Think of this as conditioning yourself to respond to situations in a positive way. Through the use of positive affirmations, you rewire yourself to create a new reality.

When you create the day with positive thoughts, you have the capacity to change yourself to become whoever you want to be.

After reading DAILY CONDITIONING, select an area to reinforce. Some days you might need to overcome fear, another day you might feel negative or there is an area to improveon. By reading and contemplating the words, it helps quiet any inner negative dialogue and begins to replace the negative thoughts with positive ones.

Keep doing this until it becomes a part of you. The key is repetition for you to own it. Think of this as mental boot camp. Over time you will be amazed as this new higher form of thinking and being becomes as natural as breathing to you.

Your daily practice should be inspirational, awaken you and make your heart sing. It is pointless if you don't feel inspired afterwards. If it comes across as unfeeling or rote, then it is not doing anything for you. You should feel ignited and have the attitude that you can do anything.

It takes 30-60 days for something to become a habit. Just like studying, you must go over the material again and again so it becomes a part of you. Just like a newly formed skill, you must practice it each day or you will lose it

Reach your Highest Potential

Let this book guide you on your path to discover and reach your highest potential. Over time you will be amazed that what you say to yourself, you are moving towards.

Reinvent Your Life in 15 Minutes a Day is uniquely written to enable you to easily grasp the concepts so they can quickly become a part of you. Use this guide in your daily practice so you can begin to think big and live a more fulfilling life.

Part One

DAILY CONDITIONING

Jump start the day by reminding yourself who you
are.   Allow the words to sink in and become a part of
you.   Let the words remind you that your greatest
achievements are still ahead of you.

At the Start of Each Day

Something good is going to happen to me today.

I am happy and grateful for everything in my life.

I expect success and abundance in everything that I do.

What I need will always show up.

I have a spiritual guide who leads me down my best path.

I know behind the scenes, things are turning around for me.

I have the insight that I need for today.

Anything is possible.

I am one step closer to my dream.

What I believe, I will see.

I see the truth about myself and all that I can be.

I am good at what I do.   I can do anything.

My inner guidance helps me throughout the day.

I see a successful outcome before it happens.

I am passionate about my life.

What I feel excited about will help me achieve my goal.

I attract opportunities to fulfill my purpose.

The Power of I Am

I am so happy and grateful.

I am at a very joyous place in my life.

I see the best in people and myself.

I have a positive attitude.

I am confident.

I know what I want.

Good things come my way.

I am at peace.

I know my chosen career path.

I know how to be happy.

I am strong and in perfect health.

I am open and relaxed.

I have everything within me to be successful.

I am in great shape and have a firm, muscular body.

People like me.

I feel good.

My life is fabulous.

I am good at what I do.

I know the rights things to say.

I can do anything.

I have a big vision for myself.

I am successful in everything that I do.

I embrace abundance.

I am in the flow and allow the Universe to help me.

* * * * *

What you tell yourself about who you are is one of the most important things that you can do.

Notice how these uplifting statements make you feel that you can do anything.

Make it a habit to do this before you head out the door each day. It's a great way to jump start the day and feel energized.

You move in the direction of your thoughts and words. Think and speak positive words about yourself.

Whatever you send out will come back to you.

More I Am's

If I believe it, I will see it.

I know the rights things to say.

I am doing better than last year.

I ask for inner guidance to help me throughout the day.

I attract opportunities to fulfill my purpose.

I am peaceful and serene.

I am born to succeed.

I am at my best and only the best comes to me.

I am being guided to the right people and places.

I am focused and accomplished.

I am a positive thinker.

I achieve great things.

I project positive energy and have a positive attitude.

I am happy and I radiate happiness.

I am what I think about all day long.

* * * * *

Get into the feelings of your words.

Remember your life moves in the direction of your thoughts and words. They have creative power.

Positive Thoughts

Anything is possible.

I am closer than I think.

I have the courage to go for it and do something else.

Money flows to me effortlessly.

I will surpass last year's income.

I give to be in the flow to receive.

What I need will always show up.

I see meaning in obstacles.

I see purpose in difficulties.

My life is shifting to attract opportunities.

I will fulfill my purpose.

I have unlimited potential.

I expect the best and the best will come looking for me.

What I seek is also seeking me.

Today is my day.

Breakthroughs and abundance are tracking me down.

* * * * *

Imagine looking up at the blue sky with outstretched arms. Feel the expansiveness of the sky. Look up at the clouds drifting by and imagine all of your problems being carried away on the clouds.

See things from a new perspective to become energized in life.

Focus on the positive to open yourself up for infinite possibilities.

Take Action

I know what I want.

I go after what I want.

I am a planner and plan to make things happen.

I follow joy and do what makes my heart sing.

I dream and have a vision that I keep in front of me.

What I pay attention to grows.

My thoughts attract like a magnet.

My desires drive me.

I move in the direction where I feel inspired.

I act on inner guidance.

I will take one small step that moves me closer to my goal.

I do what I feel excited about.

I follow up on ideas that occur to me.

What I need will always show up.

Every day I do one thing that brings me closer to my dream.

* * * * *

On your path in reaching your greatest potential, notice how alive you feel. This is confirmation you are moving in the right direction.

Follow your inner guidance. If you have an inner knowing about it and feel at peace, then keep going. You are on the right path.

Pay attention to your thoughts, desires and feelings and take action. There is no security in what is no longer meaningful. Embrace change and be open to new adventures.

What do you passionately believe in? It is human nature to maintain the status quo. Break free of the familiar to achieve new heights.

Ask every day, "What should I do today?"

Remember that action is rewarded. Doing nothing is not an option. Saying 'I don't know' stops any guidance from reaching you.

Don't wait to get started. It's time to wake up out of your sleep. You are coming into a destiny moment and great things are in store for you.

The Flow of Money

Money flows to me freely and effortlessly.

All of my needs are met every day.

Money is a positive in my life.

I handle money wisely.

I am thankful for all the abundance in my life.

I am richly paid for what I do at work.

I make it a habit to give with an open heart.

What I give comes back to me.

What I feel, I attract.

Everywhere I look money is coming in and chasing me down.

I declare a windfall is headed my way.

I come into sudden abundance.

Everything I touch turns into increasing abundance.

This is my highest income year.

I invite prosperity.

I need a miracle and I expect one.

* * * * *

Look for clues that abundance is headed your way.

Allow the Universe to guide you and take action when steps are shown to you.   Be in a peaceful flow.

Make sure the money flow circulates in both directions;

→Money flows from me →Money flows to me →

Condition your mind for wealth by imagining what you desire is already yours.

Align with the Universe

I make choices that feel right and help me grow.

I follow what makes me light up and come alive. I know this is leading me down the right path.

I take action knowing the Universe will support me. Doing nothing is not an option.

I know whatever I do, I will prosper.

My life is self-correcting. I have a self-navigation system which adjusts to keep me on the correct path. There are no wrong turns because everything is as it should be.

Every experience that I have is meant to be, to teach me a lesson and to bring me up higher. This is a powerful way to live.

I am true to myself and allow my inner guidance to show me the way.

I accept whatever is happening in the present knowing it has chosen me.

I follow joy and do what makes my heart sing.

I am a dreamer with a vision that I keep in front of me.

I move in the direction of my thoughts. What I pay attention to becomes my reality.

I know what I want and I go after what I want.

I can do anything I set my mind to do. I have everything that I need to be successful.

I feel the joy of my adventure now.

I am open to new wonderful possibilities.

I know more than I think I do.

My desires guide me on my best path to create my dream.

* * * * *

Think of the ocean as the infinite intelligence of the Universe and you are part of the ocean as a wave. Feel yourself as the wave. Feel the expansiveness of the ocean which you are connected to and all its infinite possibilities.

Happiness is a Frame of Mind

I make it a habit to be happy each day.

I believe in myself and I have everything I need to be successful.

I am happy and content.   Good things are headed my way.

No matter what comes my way, I will overcome it and come out better than I was before.

I am grateful for everything around me, no matter how big or small.

I ground myself in peaceful thoughts.

I am my own cheerleader. I cheer myself on about the progress I make towards my goals. I applaud all of my efforts.

I find something positive about everyone around me. How I think and feel towards others will return to me.

I love my life and have a fresh perspective each day.

There are treasures inside of me waiting to be discovered each day.

* * * * *

What are you saying about yourself? Make sure your inner dialogue is positive. Positive attracts positive.

Be your own cheerleader. At the end of the day applaud every little accomplishment, every little success even if everything did not turn out as well as you hoped.

Treat yourself the way you treat your best friend. Always be kind to yourself.

Intentions for Today

I intend to be happy today.

I am doing better than last year.

I am successful in everything I do.

I am transitioning to a new possibility.

I intend to be relaxed and in the flow.

I intend to enjoy life and have fun.

Anything is possible.

I meet people who assist me with reaching my goals.

Everything I need to be successful is revealed to me.

I find meaning in events and obstacles.

I expect good things will come to me today.

What I seek is also seeking me.

I sail through the day with ease and I get much accomplished.

I feel fulfilled at the end of the day.

I am ready for new adventures.

Thank You God

Thank you for the things that are coming.

Thank you for opening doors.

Thank you for prospering me.

Thank you for bringing the right people into my life.

Thank you for helping me start so you can finish your work through me.

Thank you for protecting me and turning this situation around.

Thank for working behind the scenes.

Thank you for making me a better person.

Thank you for everything that you have done and will do.

Thank you for expanding my vision and showing me the next step.

Thank you for helping me. I couldn't do it without you.

This is one of the best times of my life. I am excited about what is right around the corner.

Thank You for My Health

I feel amazing today.

Thank you for my legs, feet and toes. I am able to get around, walk and exercise.

Thank you for my arms, hands and fingers. I can pick up and hold things and do everything.

Thank you for my sense of smell. I can smell the fragrance of flowers and the clean scent of freshly cut grass.

Thank you for my sense of touch. I can feel the warmth of someone's hand and the softness of a fleece blanket.

Thank you for my gift of sight. I can see all the beauty around me and I can read.

Thank you for my hearing. I can hear the sounds of nature, birds chirping and music.

Thank you for my incredible mind. It is how I function and experience life.

Thank you for the perfect functioning of my body. Everything works together for my good.

Thank you for my good health which I am deeply grateful for each day.

Thank You for Right Now

Thank you for my loving family and close friends.

Thank you for being alive today and full of promise.

Thank you for having a grateful heart.

Thank you for all the money I have been given throughout my life.

I am deeply grateful for my job and all the people I work with.

Thank you for my income.

Thank you for my amazing car.

Thank you for the beautiful place I live in.

Thank you that I am one step closer to my dream.

* * * * *

You must be completely satisfied in the present to pave the way to a more fulfilling future.

Part Two

BECOMING AWARE

Live in the present moment and feel the magic of just being. Your life is speaking to you. Tune into its frequency and practice looking inward for answers you seek. Everything that you experience has meaning.

Tune into You

Think about yourself and your circle of influence. Every day you are showing people who you are.

Think about whom you are and your calling. What lights you up? What are you passionate about?

If you are struggling to find your passion or re-engage it, take the pressure off and simply follow your curiosity. Engage with something that interests you.

Your life is speaking to you. What is it saying?

What do you believe you deserve in life?

See yourself with a fresh new perspective.

Clear out old beliefs of what isn't possible to let something wonderful take its place.

Applaud every accomplishment no matter what the size.

Trust and believe you can accomplish anything you set your mind to. Don't try to figure things out.

Stop looking for answers out there. Look inward because the answer has always been within you.

During the idle moments real inspiration comes.

Discover and unlock the treasures inside of you.

Practice gratitude every day.

Be giving. You will receive in direct proportion to how much you give.

Abundance is everywhere. Let your heart guide you.

Being In the Flow

Being in the flow is when you are energized and connected to the creative flow and unlimited possibilities of the Universe.

The future is being created in your mind by your thoughts, feelings and beliefs about yourself. Realize that you hold the keys to your future.

Having inner peace is essential. A negative mindset, a critical spirit or resentment will keep positive things from occurring in your life. Forgive anyone who has ever hurt you. Release all negativity.

State your intention and allow the field of all possibilities to direct you to create the outcome that you desire.

There is an ease and lightness in what you are doing. You don't try to force things to happen.

Information and resources that you need pop up out of nowhere. Coincidence and synchronicity abound.

Be led by your deepest purpose. What seems easily reachable is not your best. What seems like a dream is attainable only if you follow your heart and believe it will happen for you.

Seek guidance from within. Release anxiety and any attachment to a specific result.

Create your day in advance by setting your intention at the beginning of each day.

Dream each day to open up yourself.

Having a Clear Vision

You are a walking magnet. What you put your attention on grows.

Focus on what is possible. Enlarge what you believe is possible. Your beliefs will either limit or increase you.

Live in a state of expectancy.

Have a vision of yourself and a purpose.

If there is something that you really want, then bring it to life:

- Imagine it

- Feel it

- Sing about it

- Delight yourself in it

Imagine the best possible outcome.

State what you want and feel the certainty that it will happen. This begins the process of moving in the direction to make this become a reality.

Whatever you desire, feel it deeply as if it is a reality.

For the next month, act as if you already have what you dream about.

Think BIG and see what begins to open up.

Expect good things to happen. Believe it

If your vision is not clear, then work towards something, even if you know it is not your best choice.

Taking steps will begin to open up the process and you will eventually discover your best path.

Break Out of Patterns

Set intentions each day. What do you want to accomplish or discover today?

Do things in a different way to break patterns.

Find the soul in what you do and meet each day as an adventure.

You will not live your dream if you:

- Stay in a place or a job that feels safe.

- Don't take any risk.

Be open to change. Be willing to stretch yourself and try new things if you want different results and be in a different place next year.

Embrace what is happening in the present and let the wisdom unfold.

Doors will open when you use what you have. Be open to new opportunities.

Shift your attention from the old and familiar to what is about to happen.

Engage with whatever comes your way. Your interpretation of what happens is what matters in life.

Sink into the comfort of being you and let peace and happiness radiate.

Most of life is routine so you have to change your approach to keep it alive and fresh.   What lights you up?

Do the unexpected and don't let inertia keep you stuck in place.

A Time for Transition

It's time to make a change when --

You have a nagging feeling there's more to life than what you are experiencing.

You know there is unlocked potential on the inside of you.

You feel your energy drained and you lack vitality.

There is no joy in your life.

Ideas or things keep popping up that seem important to you for reasons that are not yet known.

* * * * *

Leaving behind the security of the known to venture into the unknown is scary for most people.

Believe that when one door shuts, another door opens.

You have a bright future and things always work out for the best. Your best days are still ahead for you.

Understand deeply what you already know about yourself. All of your experiences, both positive and negative, shaped you to be who you are right now. Everything you experienced had a purpose.

Embrace change as a time to leave things behind.

When you break out of the familiar into the unknown, realize that you will be guided. You are not alone. You will begin to notice coincidences and how everything seems to be connected. You experience there is a deeper meaning to reality.

Pay Attention - A Possible Shift is Coming

Pay attention to ideas that keep popping up. Something wants to be known or created.

You should always question unhappiness. There is an underlying message for you.

What you pay attention to becomes a reality.

Ask yourself --

- Why am I noticing this?

- What ideas do I have?

- What has my attention?

- What am I here to do?

- What is my purpose?

- What step do I feel inspired to take?

- What clues are being presented to me?

- What's unfolding in front of me?

- What's important to me?

* * * * *

Look inward for answers that you seek. Everything that you experience has meaning.

Mirror, Mirror on the World

The world is a mirror of what is going on inside of you. You unconsciously create what you see.

Notice what you find attractive in others. Traits that you admire in others, you may already possess or they are in the process of developing more fully in you.

The qualities that repulse you could be aspects of yourself that you deny. If you accept this quality as part of yourself, it will no longer have a negative charge.

Relationships attract what you are. If you view yourself as damaged, you will attract damaged individuals into your life.

Everything you experience is a reflection of what is going on inside you.

You are connected to everything you see.

Pay attention to how your body feels. It signals how you are thinking.

Change in your inner world changes your outer world. Many incorrectly believe the opposite is true.

Part Three

RECOGNIZING GUIDANCE

You have an inner guidance system that is always providing messages on what is right or wrong for you. Stay on the best path for your life by recognizing its warnings when you are headed in the wrong direction.

Feelings - Stop or Go Signals

When something troubles you, you are headed down the wrong path. Change course in the direction of feeling good, which is an easy energy flow.

Pay attention to your feelings. If you feel good, then do more of what you are doing.

- What makes you come alive?

- What interests you?

- What can you do for hours and not notice the time flying by?

- What do you feel inspired to do?

- What feels easy to do?

If you follow your enthusiasm, you are on the right track.

If you feel unrest, troubled, bored or unhappy, then you are not on the right path.

- Where are you bored in life?

- Where are you frustrated?

- What drains your energy?

- What do you dislike doing?

- Where are the obstacles?

If something takes longer than expected, or there are multiple obstacles or challenges, then you are headed in the wrong direction.

Get in touch with what you are feeling when you are feeling it and then do something about it. This is more powerful than telling yourself at the end of the day that you should have done something differently.

Feeling good → then you are on the right path. → Continue with what you are doing.

Feeding bad → then something else wants to be known or created. → Ask yourself what and then do it.

Your inner guidance is always providing messages on what is right or wrong for you. Get better at paying attention to the messages and interpreting the meaning.

Check in with your body on what feels right or wrong. Your body never lies and will help you navigate through life.

If you experience neck pain, stomach ache or your stomach turns when asked to do something, view this as a big flare going up indicating what isn't right for you.

The body and its symptoms are all part of our inner guidance system. Be tuned into its language.

REINVENT YOUR LIFE IN 15 MINUTES A DAY

Feelings of Unrest or Discomfort

Have you ever experienced an uncomfortable feeling popping up when you were about to do something? Maybe it was before sending an email, making a phone call, mailing a report, purchasing something or driving down a road when a negative feeling comes across you.

If you feel:

- Unrest

- Discomfort

- Troubled

- Knowing that something is wrong

These are warnings to stop what you are doing because you are headed in the wrong direction. It's an opportunity to correct your course. Whatever you are about to do is not in your best interest or just the wrong thing to do.

Be sensitive to how you are feeling and trust your gut when something seems wrong.

I heard about a woman who took the train to NYC for a business trip. She decided to park her car at the station's parking lot and as she walked away from her car, a troubling feeling came over her. As she turned around to look back at her car, she was filled with dread.

She didn't understand why she felt this way. She rationalized to herself that every day commuters who take the train park in this lot. Believing everything would be fine; she shook off the negative feeling and continued on her way.

When she returned, she discovered her car wasn't in the parking space where she left it. Her car was stolen.

If only she listened to her inner guidance it would have prevented her from doing something she would later regret. She learned a valuable lesson that she is not likely to forget.

Remember if you are feeling good about something, then continue doing it. You are fine. It's when a negative feeling pops up, that's a clear signal to take a closer look at what you are doing because if you continue, it will not serve you well.

Although having a car stolen is a big deal, consider the warnings about little things; such as, items you shouldn't purchase. You often ignore the warning about the pants that didn't fit right or the shoes that were too tight.

It's especially important to pay attention to feelings of unrest in business. Consider the email that you were glad you didn't send because of its accusatory tone or the report that you didn't mail because you later found out it was incomplete.

Make it a practice to listen for and act upon the guidance that is given to you each day.

How Boredom Can Guide You

Boredom indicates that you need to change what you are doing,

Your inner voice sounds the alarm --

"What are you doing? I'm better than this. You have one life to live and this is how you spend your precious time doing these mind-numbing activities?"

Life can't always be exciting and much of what you do is routine. In between all the exciting and routine moments of life, begin to notice what you are doing.

Are any of the activities that are crossed off your To-Do-List moving you closer to your goals and where you want to be? If not, then it's time to make some changes.

Start with some soul searching on what you enjoy doing or a skill you would like to develop.

Pay attention to what interests you. Notice when you feel joy in what you are doing. These are signs you are going in the right direction.

When you are in sync with your best path --

- It feels right.

- There is a peace.

- It is effortless.

- Coincidences pop up that keep you on course.

When something gets your attention, it is trying to enter and become part of your reality. Welcome it.

Pay attention to signs or messages that seem significant to you. It could be a sentence you read online or in the newspaper. It could be a phrase you hear on the TV or a conversation with a friend. When you read it or hear it, something leaps out to you. You know this message is for you.

Like a detective, look for clues. Be an expert on yourself and know what clues are meant to guide you. You are connected to everything in life.

Know who you are by examining what you have created and question everything you experience in life.

Life constantly unfolds. See layers of meaning, interrelationships and coincidences. The more attention you give to this, the more you will see and understand.

Pay Attention to What Bugs You

There's a hidden message that is buried in any feelings of unrest.

I heard the story about a woman's reaction to her friend's recent marriage. When she heard the news, it was as if her world turned upside down.

Having known him for years, she observed that he always had a steady girlfriend so it makes sense he finally found the one he couldn't live without. There's a happy ending to his story and she was genuinely happy for him but why would she feel so out of sorts about this?

What she slowly realized was he didn't give up on what he wanted. He kept going, kept searching, kept putting himself out there and didn't give up on his dream.

Over the years she convinced herself that a relationship wasn't important to her but given her response, it actually was. She realized that she gave up on her dream and maybe that's what bothered her so much.

Pay attention to how you react to things. If you are troubled, don't try to deny or stuff down the unsettling feelings. The feelings are trying to tell you something about yourself, what is important to you and what could be missing in your life.

Also pay attention to what bothers you about other people. Does someone's inflated ego or emotional outbursts annoy you? If it does, then what you see as faults in others are really hidden faults in you. When you accept this about yourself and make peace with it then the negative charge will go away.

Be a keen observer of yourself. Your life is speaking to you, so learn its language and listen.

Part Four

CREATE A BIGGER YOU

There is a depth to you that needs to be rediscovered. What seems unbelievable and magical is where you are headed when you tap into the depth of yourself.

Your Life Purpose

Get in touch with who you are and your life purpose.

Turn inward and think about what gives you deep joy.

- What motivates you?

- What is the essence of you?

- What is your inspiration?

- What would make you extraordinary?

- What would you like to develop?

- What causes you to be on fire?

- What do you love?

- If you couldn't fail, what would you be doing?

* * * * *

Expand yourself and embrace what could be possible.

Organize your goals and activities around your life purpose. Each week make progress in having your life purpose a bigger part of your life.

If you need a shot of inspiration, tap into your energy source. This makes you feel better or soothed when you engage it. Try reading inspiring passages in a book.

When your life purpose organizes your life, life is not a struggle because you are aligned with your higher purpose.

Tap Into Your Source

Tap into your source to come alive. As you become an expert on yourself by becoming more self-aware, identify the activities that make your heart sing.

The following is an example to help discover your source.

I enjoy reading, learning something new and thinking about how it applies to me. The three key words are:

Reading   Learning   Thinking

When I made it a daily practice to read in the morning about self-discovery or developing my potential, I was energized and felt I could do whatever I set my mind to do.

There was a deep desire to write about what I learned over the years, so it occurred to me that I had to stop reading and begin writing.

A funny thing happened when I stopped reading. I wasn't motivated to write. Week after week, month after month passed and nothing was on paper. I doubted myself and wasn't confident that I had anything of value to write about.

I couldn't understand how I could previously be on fire to write and then after I carved out the time to write, I avoided it.

What I discovered is I unintentionally cut myself off from my source of creativity and inspiration. When I am reading, learning or thinking, I soar to unimaginable heights.

Take the time to identify what makes you come alive. Make it a daily or weekly habit to tap into it and watch what you will accomplish.

Step Into Your Higher Self

Look back at a time in your life to identify a younger version of yourself when you were:

- Truly happy

- Radiating joy

- Confident

- Positive energy

- Excited about life

What did you look like?

How old were you?

What were you doing?

What was going on in your life?

What made you so happy?

Hold on to this image of yourself in your mind and feel how you used to feel. Feel how wonderful life was and how optimistic you were about the future. Get into those feelings.

Now step into this version of yourself, your Higher Self.

Think of it as role playing the best you that ever was. Look around at everything with this new perspective. Everything feels lighter and easier.

Your Higher Self knows you, feels you and has a sense of greater possibilities for you. Your Higher Self makes you feel anything is possible.

Make it a daily practice to engage your Higher Self by asking questions. Start with, "How are you doing today?" Something happens over time which deepens the connection between you.

Step into your Higher Self and discover new possibilities.

Inner Circle of Experts

There is a depth to you waiting to be rediscovered. Use more of yourself by accessing your Inner Circle of Experts.

Think about all the things that come easy for you and areas that you excel in. For example --

- School and studying comes easy.

- You cook a gourmet meal in no time.

- Everything is organized in your home.

- You know how to troubleshoot and fix things.

- You are athletic and like to compete.

Everyone has abilities that are second nature to them. You don't even think about how you do what you do because it is just who you are.

Make a list of your Inner Circle of Experts that are within you. Some examples are –

Student	Advisor	Cook
Problem Solver	Organizer	Doctor
Planner	Detective	Teacher
Coach	Repairer	Motivator

On are regular basis, try to engage your Inner Circle to view a situation from their perspective. Use them to help you problem solve or to complete a task.

When you tap into the depth of yourself, you begin to think about things in a different way. You discover a new perspective which leads to positive energy coming from you. Everything begins to open up.

Ask your Inner Circle to help with a challenging task.

For a project at the office, if *Organizer*, *Detective* and *Teacher* are part of your Inner Circle --

- Bring in the *Organizer* to organize your thoughts and findings, plan activities and schedule meetings.

- Let the *Detective* assist with the research.

- Embrace the *Teacher* to present your findings to the group.

Once you identify your Inner Circle of Experts, make it a habit to step into their personas when you need to approach a situation from a new perspective.

Become Bigger Than Who You Are

Expand your world by doing what you normally don't do.

- Do the unexpected.

- Do something that wasn't planned.

- Give in to impulse.

- Give in to a sudden change of direction.

- Look into something that you know nothing about.

Routines set us on automatic pilot to accomplish repetitive tasks, but if that's all we do, they ultimately will constrict us. You will find the world much more stimulating when you do something new.

Be willing to change to engage life. Shed old ways of being that no longer serve you to open new pathways to transform you. The reward for your hard work is a new perspective.

Embrace obstacles and examine them. Identify the lesson that should be learned. This new way of being will set you going in a different direction.

Begin to take steps to become the person who you deeply desire to be. Trust your inner guidance and pay attention to what it wants to show you.

Whatever you are thinking about is in the early stages of being drawn to you.

Always dream and reflect on the impossible becoming possible in your life.

Dream, Dream, Dream BIG Dreams

Take the limits off yourself and dream big dreams. Tap into the wonder of a child where everything is possible.

Pretend for a moment and feel the excitement of living in your dream world.

What uplifts you, makes your heart sing and feels like you can soar higher and higher?

What seems unbelievable and magical is where you are headed if you don't stop believing. Your dreams set the navigational system in your life.

Don't give up on yourself. Dream big dreams!

When you focus on your current situation, you draw more of the same into your life. Take the limits off yourself and expand your thinking.

You are moving in the direction of your thoughts and dreams.

Everyday get into the practice of dreaming. Pretend you are living the life you dream about, even if it's only for a few moments. Do whatever it takes to get into the zone. It might be looking at pictures, listening to a song or reading something inspirational.

Remind yourself there is a bright future waiting for you.

Take Small Steps

Take small steps each day towards your goal and they will add up to something big.

Take too big a step then fear kicks in and you become overwhelmed.

The Greater the Goal → The Greater the Fear

By taking small steps, you are comfortable and you feel more hopeful.

It builds confidence when you tell yourself you are making progress and will achieve what you set out to do. Notice how empowered you feel.

Remember: A body in motion stays in motion while a body at rest stays at rest. The hardest part is breaking the inertia.

Use fear as a clue to keep moving forward. Ask yourself why it showed up and identify what you are afraid of. Don't let fear hold you back. Trust and believe things will get better.

Continue to take small steps towards your goal and don't try to force anything.

Imagine what you will say to yourself a year from now. You will be delighted that you are closer to or have achieved your goal.

Career Perspective

Find what makes you come alive and feel connected to something larger than yourself.

Your greatest abilities should be expressed through your work.

Be passionate about what you are doing and feel a sense of purpose and fulfillment.

Everything feels right and you feel like yourself.

When you immerse yourself in your work, you don't even notice the time flying by.

Successful people hold themselves up to higher standards. Have a greater vision of what is possible.

Don't be attached to a former or lesser version of who you are now.

It is exhausting trying to be someone who you're not. It doesn't work. Know who you are.

Going to work each day should feel like you are coming home. That's how good it should feel when the fit is right.

Part Five

TURNING NEGATIVES INTO POSITIVES

Embrace each challenge as an opportunity to live a more fulfilling and prosperous life. You grow in adversity so look for the meaning in each negative situation.

The Wisdom in Challenges

Whenever problems or challenges come your way, they are there to strengthen you and to teach you a lesson.

A problem is created by the Soul so you can learn by it. It's an experience or life lesson that you need to have and it will keep repeating until you master it.

My advice --

- **Let the situation change you**. You must change yourself first before the situation changes.

- **Don't resist it**. Resisting it keeps you stuck and the problem in place. Give up the struggle and things will get better.

- **Surrender to the adversity** which will get easier the more you do it. Acknowledge this is happening and look for the deeper meaning.

- **Sit with it** and allow your feelings and thoughts to show you the way. You know more than you think you do.

Everything you need is already in you. Because you are connected to a Universal Intelligence, the moment you need an answer or an idea, it will show up. Then take action.

A problem and a solution co-exist. Within the problem is the solution. Look at the problem from a different perspective.

If there are multiple problems, there is usually one underlying problem. Solve that problem to solve all of them.

Embrace each challenge as an opportunity to come up higher. The Universe is knocking you on the head to change course and do something different. A problem always indicates a turn. If you continue to ignore the warning, it will return to you over and over again.

From now on, instead of viewing difficulties negatively, view them as your personal guidance to live a more fulfilling and prosperous life.

Everything that comes into your life has a purpose and meaning,

Question your thoughts about limitations, what you think you can't do. You already have it in you to break through any barrier.

Each night before you go to sleep, ask what you need to do to solve your problem. You will be surprised by the guidance you will receive by simply asking. Trust and believe you will get the answer.

View Negatives as Positives

There is a reason for every negative situation that comes your way. View it as an unexpected opening preparing you for something new and exciting. First you must do your part to facilitate the transition from negative to positive.

- Do you need to change how you think about something?

- Are you open to change how you view yourself and your life?

- Do you need to develop in a weak area?

- Is there something that you should be doing?

- What's holding you back before you step into your greatness?

Step back and look at what lead up to your current situation. Be honest with yourself on what your part is in this.

You grow in adversity. You grow when you put a demand on your life. It's not when everything is fine or when you are in your comfort zone.

View failure as a good sign. It means you stretched yourself and tried for something.

Doors close because something better is out there.

Practice changing your reaction to the things occurring in your life. Change starts with you.

Make the most of what you have – your talent and abilities. Great things are coming your way. Use what you have and doors will open.

Focus on changing yourself then the things around you will change.

Have a knowing that things will get better.

When Negativity Knocks at Your Door

Check in with yourself throughout the day on how you are feeling. Become aware when your positive feelings suddenly turn negative.

When you are feeling negative or stressed, don't try to deny how you are feeling. This only creates more of the same negative feelings.

It's all about becoming self-aware. Become a witness to your behavior and ask yourself if there is a better way. It takes practice to catch yourself to break an engrained habit because over the years you have conditioned yourself to react this way.

You should always question why you are feeling negative. If it's something that occurs on the job, begin to identify what's going on -- what you like/dislike or what you find easy/difficult -- with your current situation. Be a detective and figure out why you feel the way that you do.

Be honest with yourself. Although it is scary rocking the security of who you are, having this clarity feels liberating. It's the beginning of a greater truth about you.

Don't try to stuff down the negative feelings and deny they exist. You are only fooling yourself and it takes an extraordinary amount of energy to do this. If you feel completely exhausted when you leave work, it could be you stuffed down negative feelings the entire day and now you feel guilty about feeling this way.

Embrace the negative feelings and stop denying who you are. This is who you are so why pretend you are anything else. Let the feelings wash over you. Don't hold on to the feelings but release them. They are here for a moment and gone the next.

Think of the negative feelings as a wave in the ocean. A wave forms and then it releases. The wave forms as you acknowledge the negative feelings and then it is released back into the ocean.

Surrender and Substitute

Are you often in a bad mood when you leave work? You know you should be happy but for some reason, you can't seem to shake off the negativity of the day.

Do you ever feel guilty because you were negative most of the day and you know better but you can't seem to help yourself?

Are you caught in a never ending cycle of negativity – you start the day feeling positive and happy only to sink lower and lower as the day wears on?

You are not alone. As you leave work, tell yourself that it's okay to feel negative. Let all the negativity, complaints, problems, not enough time with more being shoveled on your plate attitude just wash over you. Feel it, be with it and just surrender.

All this negativity is telling you something has to change but for now just acknowledge your feelings.

Don't fight them. If you try to resist the feelings, they will stick. This sounds counterintuitive, but it's true.

After you accept the negativity, switch over to something positive. One quick way to do this is to laugh at yourself. Find something about yourself or the situation to laugh about. Poke fun at yourself and don't take things so seriously or let your ego run your life.

You could sing a really silly song, the more off key the better. Try a favorite childhood song or make up your own silly lyrics on the fly to a song that you like. Are you starting to feel your energy level change from negative to positive?

Finally, think about what makes you happy. Maybe it's being with a loved one or memories of a family vacation. Whatever brings you comfort -- see it, feel it, live it, let it wash over you. As you do this, feel the happiness return.

By surrendering to the negative feelings and then substituting them with something positive is a quick way to break the cycle of negativity.

It only takes a few minutes at the end of the day for this transition to take place. A good time to try this is when you are leaving work or on the way home.

Change How You Think About It

Do you ever dread going to work each day? You tell yourself you want to do something different but walking away from your job in the short term isn't an option.

Some days you feel good about work and you wonder why you would ever want to leave. On other days you ask yourself why you are still there.

You are not alone if you experience this ever changing like/dislike attitude about your job or anything else in your life.

Chances are you can't immediately change the situation, then change the way you think about it.

What if you enjoy and are really good at problem solving and analysis, but your job requires you to do more sales which is what you dislike.

One approach is to tell yourself the reason you are contacting clients is to problem solve and analyze their situation. Turn the negative into something positive for you. You are still making sales calls but with the intention it will lead to what you enjoy doing.

Whatever you dislike about your situation, turn it into a positive.

Overwhelmed by all the emails that you must answer? Be grateful individuals think of you when they have a question and it's an opportunity for you to problem solve which is what you enjoy.

It's all in the way you think about what is occurring.

If you approach each day with the attitude of searching for the positive and downplaying the negative, then you will feel more productive and fulfilled at the end of the day.

By focusing on the positive, you attract more positive.

If you have negative feelings, don't be surprised if negative things occur. If you have both positive and negative thoughts, be aware that the negatives will begin to cancel out the positives.

Ultimately your success depends on this --

You must be happy first before you are successful in business.

Many people mistakenly believe the opposite is true.

How to Problem Solve

Actively seek the answer to your problem to allow your inner wisdom to respond.

Engage your inner wisdom by asking questions. There is an answer to your question but you must first ask the question and be open to receive the answer.

How you think about the problem can either delay or speed up the process. If you think it will take a long time, it will. If you think it is a major problem, then it is.

What you think and how you feel becomes a reality.

The problem and the solution co-exist. Be confident and have a deep knowing that you will receive the answer. Imagine that you have the solution and act as if you do.

You will find the answers to your questions in the stillness of being Practice being an observer and remain detached and at peace.

Be comfortable in the uncertainty as you wait for the solution to emerge. If you try to force things to happen, you may create new problems.

Solutions to the problem will pop up out of nowhere which will amaze you.

Creativity resides in the field of all possibilities, that anything is possible. It appears to us through quantum leaps. It is not a linear, cause and effect process.

A good time to ask for guidance is right before you go to sleep. Let your subconscious ponder the question while you sleep.

Conversation with Yourself About Stress

I want to become my best friend and look out for myself. I often look out for everyone else except me.

When I am stressed I will become a keen observer of myself.

- When did I begin feeling stressed?

- What is going on around me?

- Why am I feeling this way now?

- Why am I getting all worked up?

It could be I have always reacted this way. It's become a conditioned response that I haven't questioned.

It no longer serves me, yet I continue to do this anyway. This response has been on auto pilot and it's time to let this response go.

I will take a deep breath and imagine being relaxed. In the present moment everything is fine.

It's time to wake up and change repetitive habits that no longer serve me.

What is the reality of the situation? It could be the stressful activity is something I don't want to do and it is taking up precious time.

Time is precious because I perceive my day as not having

enough time to get everything done. With this kind of a mindset, no wonder I feel stressed.

It looks like I chose stress as my reaction to the situation.

I can break the behavior by becoming self-aware and by having a conversation with myself that there is a better way.

The key is to tune into myself.

- I will question what I am feeling. Does the reaction justify the situation?

- I will challenge myself. What is really going on?

- I will break the habitual patterns that no longer serve me.

- I will replace the stressful mindset with a peaceful thought.

- I will tell myself that I am worth this small change which will make a big difference.

Things to Say to Overcome Fear

I trust everything will work out to my best interest.

My imagined fear may not even play out so I will not dwell on negative thoughts and draw this towards me.

I will not let the storm inside of me. I will remain calm and at peace. I see myself safe and secure inside my home while a storm rages outside.

I focus on what is possible and I am excited that everything is possible.

I am comfortable in periods of uncertainty knowing a solution will emerge. I may not see it, but I know there is a solution.

Challenges will always work out to bring me up higher.

I expect good things to happen. I am blessed and happy where I am.

When one door closes, another one opens. There is something better out there for me.

My character isn't developed by playing it safe. It is developed by pressing past the fear.

I can go beyond fear and tap into my strength and settle into the peacefulness of the unknown.

Like in the Wizard of Oz, I can pull back the curtain on fear and see it for what it really is.

Everything that comes into my life has a purpose and meaning.

I've come too far to stop now. I am one step closer to my dreams.

Everything happens for a reason. God works in mysterious ways.

I am at peace because things have a way of working out.

* * * * *

Don't let fear establish a stronghold.

Fear keeps you stuck repeating the same patterns.

Fear is the belief that you cannot achieve your fullest potential.

Practice believing in yourself and don't give up hope.

When You Are Stuck

Recognize old patterns keep you stuck in old ways of being. Let go of the old to bring in the new.

Don't hold yourself back by negative self-talk and excuses that you can't achieve your dream. Don't unintentionally put yourself in a box.

Change how you think and act to achieve different results.

Break out of repeatedly creating the same unwanted experiences. Don't let the past influence how you behave today. Change your thoughts.

Examine any fear that is standing in your way with moving forward.

Recall when you overcame difficulties and how your strengths helped you succeed.

Life lessons repeat until you learn from them. Things will unfold at the right time.

Explore the depth of intelligence that is already in you. Call upon your Inner Circle of Experts in Part Four to give you a new perspective.

Let your body decide what's next. If you are too analytical, switch over to your senses for guidance. Use all of you in helping get unstuck.

Be open to all possibilities and take the steps that are presented to you.

You have everything that you need at this moment.

The moment you need an idea it will show up at the exact right time.

What you need and the people you need are close to you. The answer is within reach.

Trust that where you are is not where you are staying.

Part Six

QUESTIONS YOU SHOULD ASK YOURSELF

Engage your life by asking questions. Make it a
practice to continually ask for guidance to draw it to
you. You will be amazed at all the guidance you
receive but you must first ask.

Ask Questions for Guidance

Engage your life by asking questions. Have your life interested in you to see what comes your way. Think of it as having a conversation with your best friend.

Make it a habit to ask for guidance throughout the day. The Universal Intelligence responds to questions so to engage it, you must ask questions. Just like your best friend, give it time to mull the question over and offer possible solutions.

When you think about it, you ask yourself questions throughout the day.

- What should I have for breakfast?

- What time should I leave for the office?

- Where are my keys?

Although the answers to the above questions do not have serious consequences, what about the questions you should be asking but don't?

- Should I continue in this job that I view as a dead end?

- What should I do today to be more successful at work?

- How should I handle this situation?

- Where am I headed?

- What is the next step?

Make it a practice to continually ask for guidance to draw it to you and be on the lookout for the answer.

Pay attention to everything around you and what is trying to be shown to you.

Consider your feelings. When you feel positive, continue down that path and when you feel negative, move away.

Connect the dots and take action on the wisdom you receive. Coincidences pop up when something requires your attention.

Make it a practice right before you go to bed to ask a question about something you need for tomorrow.

You will be amazed at all the guidance you will receive but you must first ask.

Ask the Right Questions

Be mindful of the questions that you ask yourself.   Asking questions shapes your life

The right questions open you up to new ways of being and new ways of thinking about what's right for you.

- What do I want for my life?

- What is important to me?

- What makes me come alive?

- What is special about who I am?

- What is interesting to me?

- Why am I noticing this?

- What repeated thoughts or feelings resulted in this?

- What is the best way to go through this?

- What would my day look like if I enjoyed going to work?

- What should I do today that would excite and fulfill me?

- What should I do now to make this happen?

Follow the Yellow Brick Road

What is important to me? ---> This will guide you.

What interests me? ---> Follow your curiosity which will guide you.

What am I really good at? ---> This is who you are.

What can I do for hours and barely notice the time? ---> This is your unique gift.

What do I dream about? ---> This is what is in you waiting to come out.

What could I do that makes me feel happy? ---> Always follow what brings you joy.

What could I do today that takes me one step closer to my goal? ---> Align yourself with your goals and take action.

What is the lesson in this challenge? ---> This is where you need to change.

Where is the solution to this problem? --> The problem and the solution co-exist.

Where will I be one year from now? --> Take steps today to get you there.

If I was guaranteed not to fail, what would I do differently? ---> Take a chance to live your best life.

Choices You Make

As you begin to ask the right questions, practice bringing your awareness to the daily choices that you make.

Look around you and what you see today is the result of all the past choices you made. Accept your circumstances because you created them.

The future will be determined by the choices you make today. If you want to change direction, then make new choices.

Have a vision and keep it in front of you.

Ask yourself if this choice brings you closer or further away from your goal or dream. Be mindful of how committed you are in this moment.

Create a feedback loop by evaluating your past choices. Make sure your past choices are aligned with your vision. Determine if you are closer or further away from your goal.

Doing nothing is not an option. The key is to take action to get the ball rolling and see where it leads you.

Because you have a self-navigation system, there are no wrong turns, only new turns which will head you in the right direction.

With every choice you make, you are taking a small step towards something. Make it towards your dream.

Part Seven

IT'S ALL ABOUT YOUR PERSPECTIVE

Focus on all the positives in your life. Any challenges
that you faced were necessary to get you ready for
something better later on. Look at the bigger picture
for your life and believe good things are in store for
you.

Being Happy Where You Are

This is your life right now. You have what you need to be happy. Feel the joy, feel the love and enjoy everything around you.

By being completely satisfied where you are, you open up the possibility of creating something new.

Maybe your present circumstances are less than ideal. You will only move forward if you are completely satisfied with where you are right now.

Be completely satisfied in the present to pave the way to a more fulfilling future.

You are a magnet and positive attracts positive. If you think positive thoughts, you attract positive things towards you. If you harbor negative thoughts about your circumstances, you draw in more of the same   .

If your circumstances are not completely satisfying, look at them from a different perspective. Try to imagine all the positives.

If you live in a small home, tell yourself –

- My home is the right size for me right now.

- Every detail in my home is a reflection of my personal style and makes me happy.

- I can spend money on other things because my monthly expenses are lower in a small home.

If your job doesn't make your heart sing, tell yourself --

- I am grateful for the steady income each month.

- I am grateful for the company benefits especially access to quality health care and paid vacation each year.

- I am grateful I am able to build my retirement nest egg through payroll deductions.

- I work with wonderful people who are close personal friends.

* * * * *

I am grateful and happy in the two places where I spend the most time, in my home and at work.

For a Positive Mindset

Take inventory of all the positives in your life by visiting the past, being in the present and imagining the future.

Past

When faced with challenges, remember all the times when the odds were against you and you overcame the adversity.

Everything that you experienced prepares you for the future.

All of your accomplishments, all of your experiences and all of your skills will be used in unexpected ways.

Present

Be positive to attract positive experiences towards you.

Be in the moment and follow the flow on what is effortless.

Visualize the successful outcome for the day.

Dwell in enthusiasm and take action towards your goals.

It's not about knowing how, but knowing that you can.

Be kind and smile no matter what.

Embrace the present for this is where there are infinite possibilities.

<u>Future</u>

You are lucky in life and in the flow of opportunities becoming known to you.

Everything is working in your best interest to bring your desires to you.

What you long for is on its way to you.

The Law of Attraction

It's simple: Like attracts like.

- **Positive attracts positive**

- **Negative attracts negative**

You attract what you think about the most. Whatever you focus on grows in importance.

See yourself living well off and you will attract it. Whatever you identify with will be attracted to you.

If you constantly think about what you don't want, unfortunately you will attract just that.

Don't talk about difficulties in business, health or family. This will bring more of the same into your life. Talk about what you want.

If you think something new will overwhelm you or if you have self-doubts that you can do something, this will cancel out any positive intentions.

Negative thoughts, words or action will cancel out the positives and cause a delay in receiving what you desire.

Be aware when you have jealous or critical thoughts about friends or colleagues. Immediately replace the thoughts with something positive about them.

Everything you think, feel and believe is creating your future. The future is what you imagine for yourself.

Let go of limiting beliefs by changing your focus. Change negative thoughts and feelings to positive ones.

Believe you could have the life you want. What you think and feel is creating your future.

Everything is a possibility because it already exists.

You draw your desires to you by your intentions.

Take a look at what you are attracting by your intentions.

- What are your intentions for the day?

- What do you say to yourself?

- What do you believe about yourself?

Realize your feelings can strengthen the magnetic pull of your desires. The more excited you become, the more good fortune will come your way. Be in the flow.

It is not about forcing something to happen. It's about being in the flow of abundance. Tune into abundance.

If you give what you want, it will be multiplied back to you. If you are kind to others, others will be kind to you. If you want love, then give love. You must give it first to get it in return.

Be a magnet for positive things. Every day do a self-check and notice how you feel. Whatever you send out comes back to you.

Look at the Bigger Picture

Everything is working together for your good.

Don't focus on one negative experience and blow it out of portion. The negative experience was meant to happen and there was a lesson that needed to be learned.

Accept responsibility that you created everything that shows up in your life. Look for the meaning because you attracted this into your life.

If something didn't go as expected, perhaps it went unexpectedly well for reasons unknown to you.

The key is to trust this is for your good and how this fits into the bigger picture will someday be known to you.

Look back at the turning points in your life and how the challenging experiences prepared you for something better later on.

Everyday be amazed at what unfolds in your life. Everything will unfold in your life at the exact right time.

The desires of your heart are seeking you as much as you are seeking them.

Meet each challenge on the road of trials as an adventure. You never know where it will take you.

When you experience a failure, it means you tried for something and success is right around the corner.

Check Your Feelings Meter

You are a walking magnet. Make it a habit to feel good each day.

Get your feelings meter on high. Imagine you are sitting on top of the world and anything is possible.

Feel the passion behind your desires. Feel your energy level begin to increase.

Step into and imagine what you want. Imagine yourself successful and you achieved your goal. See yourself as having what you want. Feel the passion behind the thoughts.

Don't wait until you reach your goal to become excited. Feel the excitement now.

Enjoy life now by learning to have fun and feel good. Don't flat line each day.

Be grateful for everything you have and give thanks.

If you are in a negative situation or around negative people, find something to appreciate and notice how your feelings begin to change.

Your energy level attracts people and circumstances to you. Make sure it is positive.

People who believe good things happen all the time have a different frequency and energy level that attracts more good things.

Discover Your Inspiration

Take pleasure in the moment. Find the good and the magic in every situation.

Focus on experiencing life each day. It's all about what makes you feel alive.

Practice becoming more self- aware.

- What do you notice?

- What makes you come alive?

- What makes your heart sing?

Don't be passive to your surroundings. Actively look for things to love all around you.

Think about how your view on life is changing. Be grounded in the present and not hostage to the past or the future.

Slow down and enjoy the experience. If you hurry through life everything will seem like a blur.

Life is about awakening. Breathe in the new experiences and exhale the old experiences.

Be carried by your Spirit. Follow your passion to discover your gifts.

Invite what you desire to be a part of your life. Be excited and happy.

See yourself as lucky each day and know the timing is perfect to provide you with what you need.

Inspiration comes when you are not trying. Give in to unexpected urges or a sudden change of direction.

Place Your Trust in God

Everything is possible for the person who believes.

Jesus said:
Seek and you shall find.
Knock and it shall be opened.
Ask and you shall receive.

God's vision for your life is much bigger than yours.

God opens ways where you think there isn't a way.

During a challenging situation, believe God has your best interest at heart. When you are at peace, you trust God will take you through and bring you out better.

Trust and believe there is a solution to every problem. Don't try to figure it out; just trust and believe there is a way. Know God is working behind the scenes.

Take a leap of faith. Step into your power and your calling. Step forward into your greatness.

God gives you the desires of your heart. It's up to you to recognize them to bring them into your reality.

Ask God what you should do each day and to guide you. Let Him know you are listening and be on the lookout for His guidance.

Walk with your hand in God's and let peace fill your soul.

God's blessings will chase you down and will be multiplied. Be excited about the things God is bringing into your life.

Ask God to do something big in your life so you can be a blessing to others.

Thank God in advance for helping you. Let Him know that you couldn't do it without Him.

Throughout the day, make it a habit to thank God for everything that comes your way.

Find rest in God knowing all of your needs will be met.

Miracles happen every day.

Part Eight

CREATING A NEW YOU

If you want a more fulfilling life, then create an environment where you are reminded of your unlimited potential. Get into the habit of breathing life into your dreams.

Daily Ritual - Go Deep

Get into the habit of spending some quiet time each morning in meditation. If you do this upon awakening, think of it as greeting the day with an open heart.

Set your intention that today is going to be a fulfilling and rewarding day.

Daydream as often as you can throughout the day. It not only feels good but it lets your subconscious know what you expect in life.

Deeply believe that with the passage of time you will be stronger and wiser and will have an abundant and productive life. Be bold and declare you are getting younger each day.

Every night before you go to sleep, ask for guidance to any problem or situation that you will face tomorrow. You must first ask to get your subconscious to work on the answers while you sleep. Trust your subconscious and believe you will get the answers.

Sometimes answers will come to you quickly before you are even asleep so keep a pad or smartphone on the nightstand so you can capture the ideas.

Trust you will awaken with a knowing on how to proceed.

Don't Let the Storm Inside You

At the core of you is calm and peace. Give yourself time each day to gain access to your core.

Each morning put aside some time to reflect or meditate. It is in the stillness when you are receptive to fresh ideas that make your life easier.

With all the demands of life swirling around you, do not let the noise of life come roaring inside you. You chose what you let in. Imagine you are home and it is storming outside. You wouldn't open the doors or windows to let the storm inside.

It is equally important to unwind from the demands of the day and unplug. It centers you and provides a much needed window of calm and peace.

A sign of true strength is when there is turbulence all around; you chose to not let it affect you.

Throughout the day, center yourself and don't let all the upsets of life get inside you. Strive each day to live with an inner calm.

Create a Dream Book

Create a personal Dream Book of all the things you would like to have or experience.

Whatever catches your attention is a hidden desire. Start to collect pictures of what you are drawn to. If it appears in a magazine or on paper, then cut out the photos. If you find it online, then copy and paste the images into a document.

Over time you will be amazed at all the pictures you accumulated which symbolize your desires.

Maybe you discovered a Venetian Villa in a magazine and fell in love with all the windows and glass doors that open onto the balconies. You could feel how inviting the openness of the architecture is and you could imagine what it would be like to live there.

Put this in your Dream Book as well as images of different styles of gardens, flowers, landscaping ideas, outdoor pools and patios. Be sure to include the photo of the car that will be parked in the driveway.

There could be pictures of how the interior of the house will look from kitchen design and cabinetry, lighting, furniture, artwork, you name it.

You could also collect images of experiences you want to have such as vacations, running a marathon, competing in a sport, getting a degree or how about that dream job you want. Be imaginative and go for it.

When you want to escape, just open your Dream Book and take in each photo and imagine what it would be like to have these things or experiences.

Feel how your mood changes, how uplifted and peaceful you feel when you imagine what could be some day. Your life moves in the direction of your thoughts.

Focus and Begin to Dream Again

What you focus on becomes a reality.

Focus on where you want to go -- not on where you have been.

Focus on what you want -- not on what you don't want.

Focus on the fun experience you want -- then the money will take care of itself.

Use Your Imagination --

Next time you walk by an expensive car, imagine it is yours. Feel the excitement of owning the car. Imagine opening the car door and sitting on the luxurious leather seats. Imagine driving the car with the windows open, feeling the cool breeze flowing through your hair. Imagine the exhilarating experience you would have.

If it's a house that you dream about, then imagine the house, room by room. Imagine what you are doing in each room and who is there with you. Feel what it would be like to live there.

In everyday walks of life, whatever you are drawn to, whatever makes your heart sing, imagine that it is already yours. Draw it in with your imagination.

Make it a practice to see what you desire in everyday living. Think about it, feel it, be on the lookout for it. Whether it is a car, house, clothing, job, whatever it is, make a game of it and watch how you begin to attract the hidden desires of your heart.

Stir Up the Magic --

Remember as a child how you played the game of pretend. You pretended to be a fairy princess living in a beautiful castle or an astronaut who just landed on the moon. Remember the excitement when you played what seemed to be hours in your magical pretend world.

Remember how you imagined you could be anyone you wanted to be. You had a big imagination and big dreams.

Stir up that child-like magic and start to dream again. Live a much larger life and not limit yourself by your lack of imagination. Learn how to dream again each day.

How to Create Good Vibrations

When negativity comes your way, it indicates that you are being negative. Like a magnet, your negativity attracts negativity towards you.

The first step is to become aware. Notice when you switch over to negative vibrations. You feel irritated, frustrated or negative thoughts flood your mind. You're thinking of what isn't instead of what is possible. You feel stressed or have tension in your neck. These are signs you need to change your energy flow.

Stop what you are doing and find ways to feel good. It's time to create good vibrations.

If you work in an office, get up from your desk and walk around. For many, the rhythm of walking opens up possibilities. You feel lighter and more optimistic when you walk.

Listen to a song that uplifts you, that no matter what, whenever you hear it you feel better. Listen to it on your smartphone or hum a few bars to yourself. Feel the positive energy begin to come back.

Gaze at a photo of a loved one or a picture that inspires you. One inspiring picture is a person with outstretched arms standing on top of a mountain, having just finished the climb to the top. They made it, just like you will make it.

Remind yourself how great you are and that anything is possible. Review the 'I Am' and other Daily Conditioning statements in Part One to feel energized again.

Laughter is another way to activate positive feelings. You could think silly thoughts, recall a corny joke or just laugh at yourself for something you did.

It's important to think about where you are headed, not where you have been. Don't allow your current situation to have power over you. Nothing is more important than feeling good.

When you feel negative, change the way you think about it. Sometimes you can't change what is happening but what you can change is your focus so stop focusing on it.

Every day look for positive aspects about everything and everybody.

For a quick shot of good vibrations, do the following:

- Listen to a favorite song.

- Move your body or do a silly dance.

- Laugh out loud.

- Read a quote that inspires you.

- Look at a favorite photo.

- Poke fun at yourself.

- Go outdoors to gaze at the trees and flowers.

- Do something unexpected for someone.

Make it a habit throughout the day to check in with how you are feeling and take action if you need to create good vibrations.

It's Just My Imagination

What you imagine, you become.

Believe in yourself and that anything is possible.

Embrace your sense of wonder. Tap into your hidden desires.

Dream big to experience a new vision of yourself and step into your highest potential.

Breathe into your dream and give it life. Be excited and happy this is a part of you. Mentally paint a picture of your dream coming true.

You wouldn't have these desires if you didn't have the capacity to achieve them.

Here are a few methods to create an environment where you are constantly reminded about your deepest desires.

Write in a <u>Daily Journal</u> the things you want to accomplish and draw into your life.

Compose a <u>Life Purpose Statement</u> and organize your efforts and goals around it.

Create a <u>Wish Board</u> or use the side of the refrigerator for a collage of pictures and empowering words or expressions that you want to attract towards you.

Put together a <u>Dream Book</u> with pictures of all the things that you desire.

Being in the Present Moment

Be with this moment. Live in the present moment and feel the magic of just being. Experience the stillness and calm.

Take a walk to lift your spirits. Deeply enjoy the sunshine and fresh air and feel how alive you are.

Be amazed by the beauty in everything.

Be grateful for everything that you have and wait expectantly for all that the future has in store for you.

When you allow yourself to feel more joy, you will find how amazing life can be.

Embrace your child like wonder and dwell in possibility.

Do things to evolve you.

Anchor yourself in the present moment. Don't let old memories or outdated beliefs keep recreating the past.

Pay attention to what your body needs. Let your body guide you if it needs to be quiet or energized.

Put aside time each day to recharge yourself. Do something that you enjoy and be sure to relax.

Life Defining Moments as Inspiration

Think about what you already accomplished in your life. Make a list so you can see it and contemplate on what you achieved.

- Graduated from college

- Bought your first home

- Employed by a great company

- Ran a marathon

- Overcame a major health issue

- Started a new career in midlife

- Started your own business

What did it take for you to accomplish your personal list? Think about the starts and stops, the ups and downs on your journey.

- What drives you?

- What do you do when faced with adversity?

- What will you not accept from yourself?

- What ignites you at the start of each day?

See the bigger picture for your life. Identify the themes, patterns and repetitions.

One person discovered a theme of learning and discovery throughout her life. Here is Julie's story.

After graduating from college, Julie began her career in NYC. Realizing there is more to learn, she enrolled in an evening MBA program so she could continue to work full time. After getting her MBA, she was offered a new position with a Fortune 500 company.

She was successful at work for a number of years, but it wasn't the type of success she imagined for herself. There were strong feelings of discontent gnawing at her about her life.

Her health began to spiral downwards. She was diagnosed with a medical condition and was put on Medical Leave which lasted for some time.

While she was on Medical Leave, she was consumed with learning as much as she could about her condition. She suspected there might be a mind / body connection, so she became an avid reader of books about this topic.

She heard about alternative medical treatments that were practiced in Europe, so she decided to get away to try a new approach. Besides, she thought a change of scenery would do her good. During the time she was away, her health slowly began to improve.

When she returned home, she didn't want to go back to her former profession. She listened to her inner voice and realized it was time for a change and a new career. Eventually she discovered what she would do next.

Unfortunately there was a second downward spiral for her and it crashed with the diagnosis of cancer. At the time she worked for a financial firm, so she decided to put all the down time associated with medical treatments to good use and studied to get professional licenses. She succeeded and went on to get other licenses and designations and advanced in her career.

Let's stop here with her story. Look at the theme of learning in her life and how it transitioned her to the next step. Learning and discovery are what saved her when she hit rock bottom. They are the core of who she is and she can always rely on them to get her through difficult times.

Think about what it took you to get to where you are today.

Think about all the challenges you had to overcome. What was present that helped you push through the obstacles?

Think about all the times when everything came together and you felt like you were sailing though life. What was present?

What gives you the determination to go forward, to meet each challenge head on, and not give up on your dreams?

Spend some time to identify your core and what you can always rely on to get you through difficult times.

Use your life defining moments in your personal story as inspiration when you are faced with what seems to be impossible challenges.

CLOSING THOUGHTS

It takes practice and determination to break long standing habits and ways of thinking that no longer serve you. The reward for all the hard work is a new and improved you. As you endure all the ups and downs in life, you will have a deep knowing that everything was meant to bring you up higher.

Everything happens in life for a reason. As you develop the ability to look beyond the immediate circumstances, you discover the deeper meaning intended for you.

Experience how everything begins to open up and life becomes a little bit easier and lighter. Getting to a new higher level of thinking and being is a process. Be committed and practice, practice and then practice more so it becomes a part of you that you can't live without.

Turn to this book each morning and let the words sink in and uplift you. Over time you will find this new script will become automatic and you will be well on your way to reach your highest potential.

Get your friends and loved ones involved with this new way of being and be sure to plug into ways that reinforce these concepts. Check out Joel Osteen's TV broadcasts and free podcasts. His inspirational messages are a personal favorite of mine.

Be excited that you are well on your way to reinvent your life and be the best you that you can be!

ABOUT THE AUTHOR

Suzanne Wescoe is passionate about being true to herself by following her deepest desires.

Her book is the culmination of years of reading and research. The inspiration for the book was her small spiral notebook with handwritten notes of concepts that she wanted to embrace. Each morning before she headed out to the office, she would spend 15 minutes reading over the passages which ignited her with a positive mindset and an anything is possible attitude.

Over a period of time she discovered that many of the concepts became her automatic response to situations. She realized that by simply reading the notebook each morning she was rewriting the script for her life.

Her work is published in this book so it could be shared with people around the world.

She has 16 years of professional experience in financial services. As a CERTIFIED FINANCIAL PLANNER™ professional, she counseled clients on how to reach their personal financial goals. She has a MBA from Rutgers University.

Printed in Great Britain
by Amazon